Isaac Kimbal Felch

The Breeding and Management of Poultry

Thorough-Breds for Practical Use

Isaac Kimbal Felch

The Breeding and Management of Poultry
Thorough-Breds for Practical Use

ISBN/EAN: 9783337144692

Printed in Europe, USA, Canada, Australia, Japan

Cover: Foto ©Andreas Hilbeck / pixelio.de

More available books at **www.hansebooks.com**

THE

BREEDING AND MANAGEMENT

OF

POULTRY;

OR

THOROUGH-BREDS FOR PRACTICAL USE.

BY

I. K. FELCH,

NATICK, MASS.

HYDE PARK
PRESS OF THE NORFOLK COUNTY GAZETTE.
1877.

PART I.

INCUBATORS

AND THE

ARTIFICIAL REARING OF CHICKENS.

That poultry husbandry has become one of the largest of our productive industries, is now quite generally appreciated and admitted.

Its capabilities, however, have not yet been dreamed of, for when the artificial hatching and rearing of chickens in large numbers have been proved practicable to the people generally, there is actually no limit to the extension of this industry. The demand for early chickens among the hotels, restaurants and wealthy families of our large cities is immense, and it is constantly growing. The supply is entirely inadequate even at the highest prices, and the field for remunerative labor in this direction is very broad. There are thousands of persons of limited means, who, provided they were supplied with a perfectly reliable incubator, could at a very small outlay of capital and labor add to their means very materially and surely. Such labor as would be required in this industry would be of the very lightest, and could be performed easily by women and even children. In fact, we know of nothing else among the varied interests of rural life that could be made so *available to all* as the artificial rearing of domestic poultry. In addition to its use in hatching chickens for market purposes simply, an incubator is a prime necessity to the fancier and poulterer.

Who has not desired to get out his chickens early, yet has been disappointed either by the lack of sitting hens, or by the method of sitting of those he had secured. Who has not lost many clutches of eggs from his choicest birds ; eggs that to him were almost priceless, because he had no incubating hen or machine to receive them at the critical time.

In our opinion the autumn exhibitions and sales might be vastly enriched by great numbers of early hatched, well developed birds, provided a perfectly practicable and reliable incubator were available.

It is not our intention to devote much space to a review of all that has been done in the way of artificial incubation abroad and at home. Neither is it our design to describe the many clap-trap machines that have been invented and sold in this country to the great disgust of the buyers. We venture to say there are more worthless incubators scattered throughout the country, packed away in garrets or cellars, and held by their disappointed owners as so much trash than there are of all other condemned machines.

That such is the case, proves there is a want for a good and reliable incubator among all classes, and it also proves that such has not yet been supplied.

The fact is, no incubator is of any value whatever, unless it contains within itself every principle, every phase, and every condition that nature furnishes for the incubation of the egg and the successful hatching of the chick.

In order that such an incubator should be created it is first necessary that the egg and the embryo should be studied in all the stages and wants of its existence.

The egg is one of the most beautiful of created things. It is, although apparently so simple, wonderfully complicated yet entirely complete.

To the careless observer it consists of but two elements within the shell, the yolk and the surrounding albumen. Yet the careful student finds within these a multiplicity of features and conditions quite beyond the vision of the ordinary experimenter.

Now to study an egg requires a trained hand and eye. It also requires in the student, a knowledge of anatomy and a skillful manipulation of the microscope.

As the embryo chick advances in growth and perfection, it is necessary that every phase and requirement of its embryohood should be studied and understood.

Professors Huxley, Agassiz, Foster, Balfour, Bischoff, Dollinger, and Karl Ernst Von Baer, have devoted years to the study of the egg, and to their scientific labors we owe most of our knowledge of embryology.

Their studies were confined entirely to the physiological life of the chick, and none of them pursued their labors to an utilitarian end; that is, they worked as scientists, not as inventors.

We have said that no incubator is of any value unless it contains within itself every condition that nature furnishes for the successful hatching of the chick. As a rational deduction from this, no one can invent a successful incubator, unless he fully understands what those essential conditions are.

It is very rarely that a scientist is a practical or mechanical inventor; the requirements of the two are so radically opposite, that they are not, as a rule, combined in the same individual; fortunately there are exceptions to this rule.

Among the many incubators that we have examined, we take great pleasure in naming that invented by Mr. Edward A. Samuels of Waltham, Mass.

This gentleman is well known throughout the country as a naturalist, and one of his books, the Ornithology and Oölogy of New England, is regarded as standard authority. For many years he has been a close student of nature, and his schooling in this direction would apparently fit him for a study of any of the phenomena of animated life.

Some eight years ago he commenced the study of the egg and the chick, and to facilitate his work, he made an artificial incubator. It was of course a rude affair, but it would hatch seventy-five per cent. of the fertilized eggs placed within it.

The idea at that time, of inventing a machine for general use, never, we believe, occurred to him. In fact, until recently, he has made no effort in this

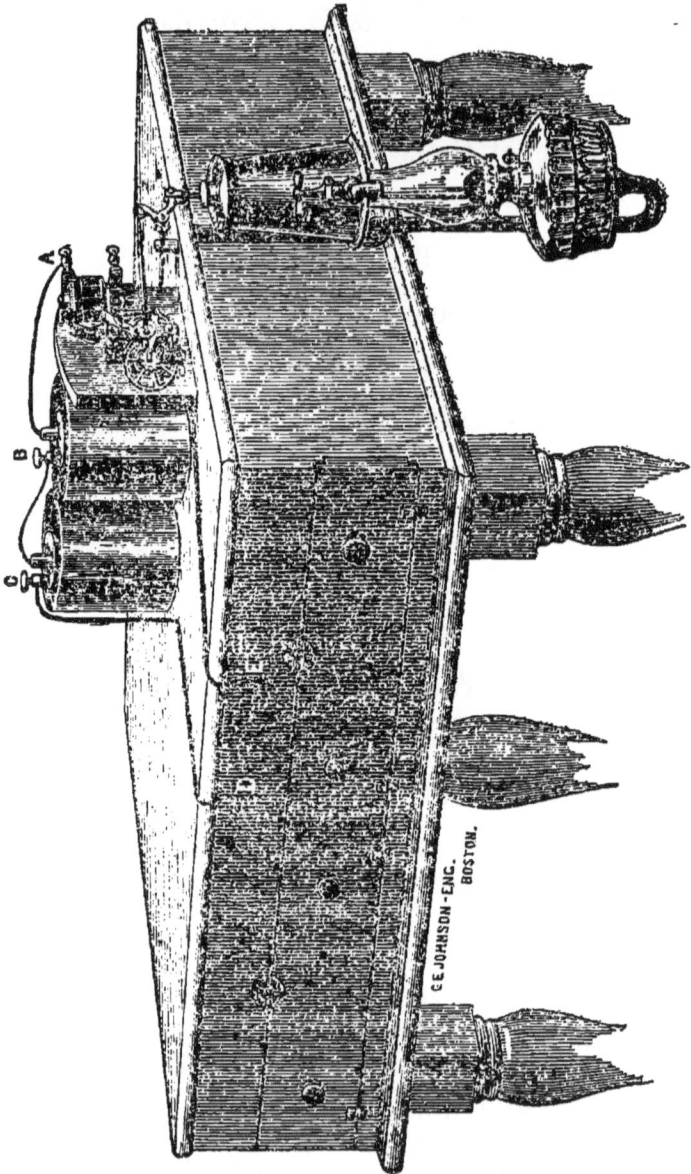

THE ECLIPSE SELF-REGULATING INCUBATOR.

EDWARD A. SAMUELS, Patentee and Manufacturer,

WALTHAM, MASS.

Fig. 1 gives an illustration of the front and the boiler end. The doors open down to permit the drawing out of the egg drawers. The battery, clock work and lamp in actual use are arranged as here shown.

line whatever, and we believe, we were among the very first to suggest it to him. In compliance with this hint, Mr. Samuels has, in the course of his studies and experiments to perfect a machine practicable for common use, used many thousands of eggs, and constructed almost innumerable forms of incubators; the result is he has elaborated a machine that is perfectly reliable and practical, and withal one that follows nature as closely as can be done.

In an incubator it is essential, first, that it shall maintain automatically a uniform heat, which shall be so controllable that it may be regulated, or rather self-varying, according to the advancement made by the chick. Second, it shall furnish its own ventilation and moisture.

These are absolutely all the essentials in a machine to be successful.

To ascertain the requisite degree of heat, Mr. Samuels took numerous observations of the temperature of the upper surface of the egg beneath sitting hens, three times daily through their whole terms of incubation.

His thermometer was one of the most sensitive obtainable, and though the hens were sitting under various conditions, the average heat in the different specimens was about the same, and was greatest at the commencement of incubation and least at the close. A fact, by the way, quite in conflict with the theory held by many persons both in this country and in Europe.

The proper degree of heat ascertained, it was necessary first to secure a uniform circulation and distribution of it *above* the eggs.   All who have had any experience with incubators know their heat is not radiated uniformly upon the eggs, those in the middle being quite hot, while those on the edges are almost cold, too cool in fact to permit their hatching.

In order to secure the proper uniformity, a great many forms were made, tested, and cast aside until at length the best form was arrived at.   All this required a large outlay of time and money, but nothing was permitted to stand in the way.

After the right degree and uniformity of heat were attained, it was necessary that it should be made controllable automatically, or so self-regulating, as to follow the various needs of the embryo chick ; that is to say, it was to be so made that it would not only regulate its heat automatically for the time being, but it would follow the process of incubation, giving less and less heat as the time drew near for the chick to be hatched.

After many disheartening trials, he, by the combination of a small electric battery and a clock-work, finally succeeded in securing this important result. The moment the temperature within the incubator reaches a certain point, an electric circuit is closed by an ingenious pyrometer attachment, and this operates on an electro magnet, the armature of which instantaneously moves to the magnet; in thus moving it releases the escapement of a clock movement, causing a ventilator to open and the flame of the lamp which furnishes the heat to be reduced to the minimum point. When the heat in the incubator is sufficiently reduced, the electric current is broken, the ventilator closes, and the lamp again burns up brightly. This is absolutely automatic, and it is strictly reliable.

To secure the proper ventilation and moisture, Mr. Samuels tried many plans, rejecting all until a successful one was obtained.

To show how thoroughly the work has been done we will give as an illustration, a single incident. He had perfected his incubator, as he at one time supposed, had secured a perfectly automatic control of it, and the heat and moisture were of the proper degree, yet the chicks did not hatch in anything like the proper percentage. A few came out, but most of them died after the fifth day of incubation. At that time perfect ventilation of the eggs had not seemed requisite, and it was only after proving beyond a doubt that it was at and after this stage of the embryo's existence that pure air should be supplied in proper quantities, that an entirely new model was tried and adopted.

The blood of the embryo chick is oxygenated through the myriads of pores in the shell of the egg; the sitting hen often rises to turn her eggs, and whenever she moves fresh air has access through her feathers to the embryos beneath her. Mr. Samuels tested chemically, the air in one of the incubators, (such as I have said he discarded,) full of eggs, and found carbonic acid gas in deleterious quantities; the embryos had died from imperfect aeration of their blood.

The apparatus that he has at last perfected is, as we before stated, automatic, and it is so perfect in its working that he has hatched recently as high as eighty-five per cent. of the fertile eggs placed in it. We may therefore call it a success.

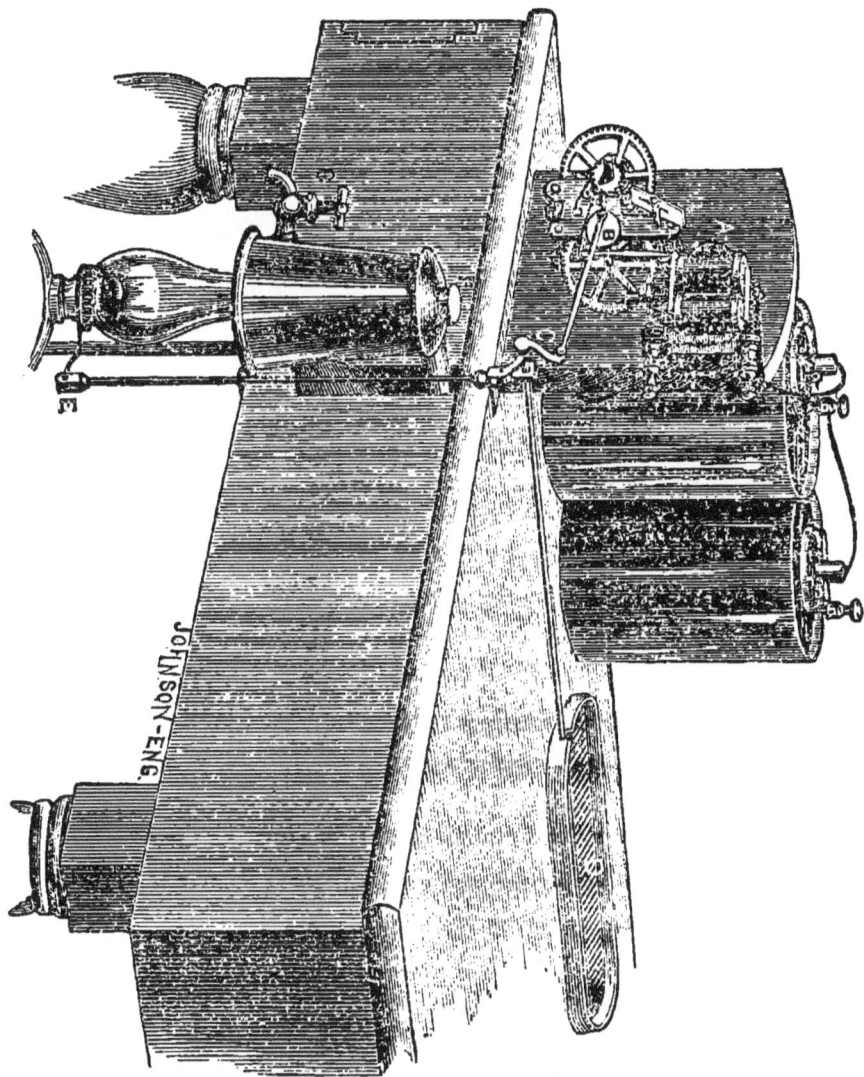

THE ECLIPSE SELF-REGULATING INCUBATOR.

Fig. 2, Side View.

EDWARD A. SAMUELS, Patentee and Manufacturer,

WALTHAM, MASS.

It is as we understand now patented, and the manufacture of it has commenced. It can be sold, as we are informed, for $60.00 for an incubator large enough to contain three hundred eggs.

This price, as it includes the incubator, battery, pyrometer, lamp, and everything complete, is very low, and as it is within the reach of all we predict for it a large sale.

The labor and supervision required in running it are quite limited. The clock work needs winding up once in two or three days, three turns of the key being sufficient. The lamp needs filling once in twenty-four hours. The battery requires once in a fortnight or so, the addition of a gill of water according to the evaporation. There is no turning or sprinkling of the eggs needed.

It may be readily seen from this that the care required, is hardly greater than would be necessary in managing a single sitting hen, and we doubt if there is any possibility of anything like a successful incubator being invented that would call for less attention.

That the successful hatching of chickens artificially has been proved beyond a doubt, and that they may be reared in large numbers in a limited space without the assistance of mother hens, Mr. Samuels, and many others have also demonstrated.

To raise the many chickens hatched in his incubators in the course of his experiments, Mr. Samuels constructed a house 90x15 feet in dimensions, and of a height of nine feet at the front and five feet at the rear. It faces the south, and the front and two ends are of glass, the roof a lean-to shingled, and the back clapboarded.

In this house he placed a green-house boiler large enough to heat it, and he adjusted the hot water pipes which were four inches in diameter so that the young chickens could brood beneath them. Of course the pipes were wrapped with blanketing, or other woolen material, and above them was fixed a board covering from which were pendant strips of buffalo skin or woolen cloth for the chickens to creep under. When they were brooding beneath the pipes they were as warm and comfortable as they could possibly be beneath a hen. The cost of house, boiler, and everything complete was about $500.00 The proper degree of heat being thus provided, all they required was absolute cleanliness, a variety of food, a good space of clean gravelly sand for their walk, and there was no difficulty in raising many hundreds in the dead of winter, in the small area we have named.

An absolute necessity to chicks reared thus is that one meal a day, of green food, should be furnished. To supply this he sowed oats and winter rye in a part of his chicken house, and as fast as it was used another seeding was made.

In this house Mr. Samuels had at one time seven hundred chickens of all ages, from those just hatched, up to pullets laying and even wanting to sit.

When we state that these chickens were brought up in flocks of 30 or 40, in pens 6x15 feet to each flock; that they had never been out of these pens, and that they were in perfect health, we think it is shown conclusively that the thing is practicable and that any one may do it under the same conditions.

All poulterers have heard of the mammoth establishment of Mr. Baker in New Jersey in which thousands of chickens are reared artificially for the early market, and many are acquainted with the methods practiced in England and Continental Europe. Now it is not every one who has the means or the inclination for entering into the business on these large scales, and we would say here that the thing is practicable in as small a way as one wishes. All that the chickens require is to be kept absolutely clean, that they shall have a warm place to brood in whenever they wish, and their food shall be nutritious and varied.

We have known of instances where hundreds of chickens have been reared during a winter when the only brooding facilities afforded them consisted of several wooden boxes lined with flannel or woolen carpet or old buffalo skin, the boxes being placed near a stove at night, and in severe weather. There are many farmers who rear all their spring chickens in this way, and some of them sell several hundreds of dollars worth every year. There is absolutely no obstacle to the successful prosecution of this work, provided always that the chickens are given the proper treatment. *If they have warmth, cleanliness, freedom from vermin, gravelly sand to run on, a variety of food and a daily supply of either chopped grass, oats, cabbage or lettuce, they may be raised in any number desired.* These conditions are absolutely essential.

There can never be an artificial mother invented that will equal the mother hen, and when we con-sider the many failures of the hen to hatch her eggs in the early part of the season, we can see of what value such an incubator as we have described will be, for it makes every hen, inclined to sit, of far more than double her original value, for she can be furnished chicks to rear of double the number she would be able to hatch, and in cases of failure to hatch, a full brood of twenty to thirty chicks can be supplied for her to rear. There is no artifical heat to compare with the breast and feathers of the hen.

In leaving this chapter of our subject we offer in substance our Essay before the Massachusetts State Board of Agriculture. It is our idea of practical poultry keeping, and we believe that if its instructions are heeded, no better guide to the Farmers and Poulterers of the land, can be given. The colonization system as therein advised will be found the best one to follow, and it adapts itself to the small or large operator alike.

PART II.

MAGNITUDE AND MANAGEMENT;

AND

DISCUSSION OF THE BOARD UPON THE SAME.

ALTHOUGH the poultry interest of the nation has been considered of minor importance, yet when we investigate, we find the egg and poultry product to be much larger than any other agricultural product or industry, and we become amazed at the amount of wealth annually accumulated by practical poultry keeping.

The census for 1870 informs us that the cotton crop was 3,011,996 bales; the corn crop, 761,000,- 000 bushels; the wheat crop, 288,000,000 bushels; the value of all the cattle, sheep, and swine slaughtered or sold to be slaughtered was $398,956,376;

the hay crop, 28,000,000 tons, valued at $14 (a high estimate), was $384,000,000.

The assertion that the egg and poultry produce of the States exceeds either of these large products, is met with derision ; yet it is true, and the produce finds no rival save in the entire meat and dairy product combined.

Compute the nine millions of families in the States as consuming but two dozen eggs per week, and ($20) twenty dollars' worth of poultry per year, and we have (computing eggs at twenty-five cents per dozen,) over $405,000,000. Nor is this all. Large as it is, to it must be added the consumption by the saloons, restaurants, confectionery establishments, our thousands of hotels, together with the medicinal and chemical and exportation demand, which will swell the amount to not less than five hundred millions of dollars as the annual product of the United States ; an interest worthy of our considerate investigation. When we commence to make figures, we become surprised at their magnitude ; and that you may not underrate the hotel consumption, we will say that a New York innkeeper offers sixty cents per dozen for three hundred dozen of eggs per day, if he can find the party who will guarantee their delivery fresh ; and this is for the demand of three hotels only. The consumption of meat to each guest per day at the Grand Pacific, the proprietor of the hotel informs us, is $2.50, and two-thirds of that amount is for poultry and game. Another item should be considered in this connection, and that is, thousands of prairie farmers, who live so remote as to make the running of meat-wagons unprofitable, are obliged to rely on their farms for fresh meat, and it is a fact that two-thirds of it is poultry and eggs. It is the custom with them in early winter to kill and pack in snow and ice the supplies of poultry for home use. This, with the richer third of the population who consume far more than the estimate offered, will more than make up for the poor of our Eastern cities, who consider poultry a luxury and seldom indulge in its use. With these items as data, we claim our estimate of five hundred millions to be far less, rather than more than the actual yearly product, which as we have said, makes the industry of poultry breeding and keeping one of the largest in which our farmers are interested. Like in comparison as the giant oak to its acorn origin, is this large product, made up from the small collections from the small flocks of fowls seen about the door of the hamlet and the farmhouse, in numbers of 12, 20, 30, and 50, and where a larger number is seen so rarely that they become the exception. These flocks pay a large profit on their cost of production, as may be seen by consulting the different societies' reports. In 1858, we see that thirty-eight fowls, kept in small yards, under unfavorable circumstances, with a market at thirty-eight cents for corn, sixteen and two-thirds cents for eggs, and fifteen cents per pound for poultry, yielded a net profit of $1.38 per head. In 1861, Mr. Mansfield's experiment with one hundred hens, having a free range of the farm, consuming but ninety-three bushels of corn or its equivalent, produced one hundred and forty-seven eggs each (no chickens being raised that year), and yielded a net profit on eggs alone, of $1.35 per head; to which, had the value of the guano been added, the figures would have reached the sum of $1.60. These, and other statements, are to be found in the Middlesex South Society's reports, of $2, $2.25, and $2.50 per head profit per annum; and last, but not least, the banner statement of Mr. Whitman in 1873. With fifty-one Leghorns, which laid two hundred and seven eggs each, which he sold for thirty-one cents per dozen, the cost of keeping the fowls being $1.13 each, he shows a profit of $4.04 per head, proving conclusively that these small flocks pay much better with care than do other farm stock.

All the different breeds will pay a handsome profit if furnished quarters suitable for their condition, and properly cared for; and, generally, it is best for the breeder to make a specialty of the kind his taste shall dictate. But with our twenty years' experience with all the so-called thoroughbred varieties, we are led to advise, that, taking into consideration the individual merit and associate worth, the selection of Light Brahmas, Leghorns, and Plymouth Rocks, for they will be found to pay the best for extra care.

The Brahma is a superior winter layer, producing the larger number of her eggs from October to May. As poultry, the chicks have to be killed quite young, — say eight to ten weeks old, as broilers; the most profitable time, as roasters, being at eight months. This makes them late as poultry; but to make up for it in a measure, the virgin cocks are tender enough for roasting at even twelve to thirteen months, more so than the native at seven or eight months, and in early spring, sell next in price to capons.

The Plymouth Rocks are good average layers, and excellent mothers, their special merit being that they are rapid growers, and make fine poultry for summer and early fall; and so long as the breeders are content to have them fill this middle ground between the small and the Asiatic breeds, so long will they grow in public favor, and remain one of the three best breeds for the farmer's use.

The Leghorns are a non-sitting variety, and one of the largest producers of eggs, being most prolific during the warmer months of the year. Their chicks make nice early, though small broilers, and should be killed as such; for, as roasters, their skin is tough and carcass too small, their chief merit being in egg production alone. They are very quick growers, many pullets commencing to lay at four months and a half old, and there are cases on record in our own yard, where they have laid at three months and three weeks old. We have also started with eggs and produced three generations in three hundred and sixty-three days. This precocity enables one to raise his stock-birds even after the season is too far advanced to rear successfully the

Plymouth Rock or Brahma. Thus you see how peculiarly adapted one to the other the three breeds are, and all of them are hardy, standing much neglect. With them, the farmer easily caters to the wants of the markets the year round.

With the above breeds as stock, the yearly product will average one hundred and fifty eggs and eight chickens to each hen, which will sell (taking Natick market for 1875, as a basis), as follows :—

12½ dozen eggs, at 25 cts. per dozen, . . .	$3 12
4 pairs of chickens, 28 lbs., at 25 cts. per lb., .	7 00
American guano, ...	25
Total, ...	$10 37

The cost of producing the same being,—

Keeping of hen, ...	$1 15
15 eggs for incubation, ...	38
Cost of growing 8 chicks to 35 lbs. live weight, at 9½ cts. per lbs., ...	3 32
Interest on investment and casualties, . . .	60
Total, ...	$5 45

To notice some of the other breeds, we will say, " the Hamburg family" is one of merit as egg producers, yielding about one hundred and sixty-five eggs per year, as a rule; and there is a case on record where a single hen of the Golden-Spangled variety laid one hundred and fifty-one eggs in six months. As poultry, the meat and bones are dark, so much so as not to be desired by market-men. The race is delicate, and hard to rear, but when six or eight months old, seems to have become quite hardy, except it be a predisposition to the disease called "black comb," — but why the disease should be so termed we cannot understand. To be sure, the comb turns black, but the causes come from derangement of the egg-producing organs. We have seen them lie down, their combs become black, and they, to all appearance, dead, when all at once they would expel the egg, and in a few moments they would be singing about the yard as well as ever.

The different varieties of this family are Golden-Spangle, Golden-Pencilled, Silver-Spangle, Silver-Pencilled,—this last being the old-time Bolton Grey, under which name it was first imported into this country. The white and black varities are of more recent date than the first four named ; the black, we think, the most hardy and prolific of them all.

The Spanish was long known as one of the best layers, and, in fact, the old Minorcas were in every respect equal to the Leghorns, but the breeding of the white face upon this breed has resulted in the fact that much of their merit has been sacrificed.

Their eggs are larger than those of any other breed, but in number they fall much behind the average. They are extremely delicate as chicks, but when once matured, they seem reasonably hardy; and the contrast of a pure white face and ear-lobe, with their metallic, green-black plumage, makes them much admired. As poultry, here in America, we would not concede, perhaps, that they were up to the average. Their dark legs and white meat are not preferred by the masses.

The Dominique is every way equal in merit as to number of eggs, and in poultry equally as good, as the Plymouth Rock; it being rather under size, compels it to take a second place. In all other points, what has been said for the Plymouth Rocks, would apply to the Dominique.

The French class, comprising Houdans, LaFleche and Creve Cœur, while they are highly appreciated in France, have failed to give general satisfaction in New England. But Mr. Aldrich of Hyde Park has been successful with the Houdans, and claims for them all that is excellent as table fowls, besides being a good average producer of eggs : they are more inclined to non-sitting than otherwise. But the Houdan and Creve Cœur require warm, dry quarters. They, like the Polish, are inclined to roup if confined in damp quarters.

The La Fleche are the most delicate to rear of the whole class, and in our northern climate are much troubled with a weakness in ther limbs. A good healthy hen of this breed, we believe, will lay more eggs from March to October than any other breed, not excepting the Leghorn.

The Cochins are, in England, much preferred. They are good mothers, being covered with long, fluffy feathers. They are hardy, and as layers in winter are hard to excel. Their eggs are furnished with a thick shell, and in closely bred birds are extremely hard to hatch. There are the Partridge, Buff, White, and Black varieties, all having their admirers; the Partridge being the most beautiful, while the Black has undoubtedly the most merit, for they are good layers and fine poultry. For one dollar, the " American Standard of Excellence" can be obtained, which gives a full description of the different breeds. We therefore omit description of breeds in this essay.

As a rule, a bushel of corn will produce nine pounds of live weight in poultry, and, with good even care, one has only to weigh his chicks to know their cost. When fowls are fed sparingly, being kept short, they become an expense ; for there is no stock that pays so poorly, if neglected, or as well, if extra care is taken of them. A greater profit will be realized on incubating breeds, if allowed to rear one brood of chicks during the season ; for the incubating season gives the laying functions rest, and you get more eggs, we are confident, in the year, beside the care of the brood of chicks gratis ; and as the chicks will pay one hundred per cent profit on their cost, you will find that many of the incubating breeds will pay as well, and even better, than some of the non-sitting varieties. In all breeds, it will be found to pay to take pains to make your selections from the best-laying families of the breed, for there is as much difference in them as there is in the Shorthorn breed of cattle for milk.

The smaller the flock, the greater will be found the individual yield ; but the most economical provision, taking into the account the care of the flock and greatest comparative profit compared to cost of provision made for them, will be found in groups of fifty, for a greater number will not do as well together. This number can be kept in health and a high productive condition in a house with a laying-room fifteen feet square, an open shed ten by fifteen, posts seven feet high, all under one roof, which can be half-pitch, with a cupola-ventilator twenty inches square. The exhalations from fowls are very poisonous, and it is very essential that they have thorough ventilation. At the same time, we must not expose the flock to a direct draught of air. Fowls, left to themselves, will not stand in a draught, and, when compelled to, they take cold as easily as does the human family.

A window on the south side of the laying-room, six feet long and four feet wide, the sill of which comes down to within one foot of the floor, will warm and light the room, and keep the gravel dry, which will help in the work of deodorizing the droppings. Construct a platform twenty inches from the floor, twenty-two inches wide, around the walls of the room. One foot above the same, place the roost, which should be two and a half, and, for Asiatics, three inches wide, — the corners rounded off. Under the platform construct the nests by means of a portable frame that will be fourteen inches deep, the front made of two strips five inches wide, and a door nine inches wide, which is to be let down to gather the eggs. This will give a passage-way of eight inches in the rear, thus making smooth work in front and giving seclusion to the nests, —the same being easily removed to cleanse them. Avoid all permanent or box-made nests, which become harbors for lice. Avoid, also, the old plan of an inclined plane for roosts, for all the fowls will strive to occupy the highest perch, and many a fight and fall will be the result, which will vastly increase the list of casualties, while the low and level plan saves many from lameness and internal injury; for while a hen will walk up to her perch, if she has the chance she will invariably fly down. Roosting low makes them less breachy; even the smaller breeds, if reared on low perches, will not require a fence more than four and a half to five feet high to fence them in. The floor of the house should be kept covered three to four inches deep with a coarse-fine gravel, not so fine as to be called sand, yet having a loam mixture in it. This will deodorize all the filth and stench — the bane of the poultry-house.

The floor should be raked over at least three times each week (if it cannot be done daily), and all surface filth, with the droppings from the platforms removed, and the whole replaced with a fresh supply

of soil twice each year. The fertilizer thus manu-
factured will be found excellent for all root-crops,
especially onions and carrots.

If the flock is to be confined, and on the least
practical amount of ground, each house and shed
will need two yards, two rods wide and ten rods
long ;. the two being necessary, so that while one is
in use the other can be sowed down to forage crops,
thus furnishing the fowls with raw vegetable food,—
as much a necessity as grass for the cow, to secure
the best results.

In constructing these conveniences for your fowls,
do not think you can get along without the open
shed, for experience teaches that for a large production of eggs and security of their hatching when set,
that the fowls must have the open air daily ; and a
shed that protects them from the storms and driving
winds in winter, and furnishes cool retreat in summer, will prove a most judicious expenditure. These
numbers and fixtures can be augmented to any num-
.ber required, but each fifty should be a community
of itself. Add no more than you can care for as
well as you do the first fifty you start with, and on
which you have based your calculation of success.
The many failures are to be attributed to neglect, and

failure to care for the many, with a generosity corresponding to that given the first few.

The feed for fowls thus confined may consist of boiled vegetables (purslane, cabbage, squash, seed-cucumbers or potatoes), mashed with wheat-bran and corn meal, while hot; feeding the same at the morning meal in such quantities as will be eaten up by nine o'clock, allowing the flock to forage till four or five o'clock, when a full feed of small grain and a small portion of corn may be fed to them, adding to the morning meal fresh ground scraps or meal in some form, three days in each week. This will be found sufficient till the frost prevents the further growing of forage crops; then change the feed to what soft food they will eat up at the morning meal, — small grains, sunflower seed, etc., at noon, and what corn they will eat at evening. This will maintain the most even animal heat for the twenty-four hours; it being health and heat that produce the eggs, the hen being simply a machine which, if carefully run, must produce the egg or die. During the winter months, feed chopped cabbage and turnips, and rowen hay. Rowen clover is an excellent substitute for grass, and is the only thing we can find that will produce eggs that will make the golden sponge-cake and custard like that seen in summer. They will eat from five to six pounds per head during the winter, if fed in a rick, keeping them constantly supplied; and while it increases their productiveness, it also increases the beauty of their plumage, making it well worth one's trouble to supply the same.

The cost of keeping as above will be found to be from $1.15 to $1.25 per head. The construction of such quarters, as described, and the purchase of natives or grade stock, will cost from $2.50 to $2.75 per head, or if a start be made with thorough-breds, $5.00 per head as capital invested.

In this connection, we would like to call your attention to the many natural facilities now unimproved, by which the number of eggs would be increased, and a portion of the food and a large per cent. of the outlay described, be saved.

There is no reason why fifty fowls to the acre could not range with the cattle in our pasture-lands, and both land and cattle be benefitted thereby.

When thus colonized, it is noticeable that certain fowls adhere to certain members of the herd, busy in catching the flies that pester them, and consuming the worms and insects disturbed by grazing.

In most of our pastures there are dry knolls and southern sloping hillsides, in which excavations could be made fifteen by twenty-five feet, the ends and north sides walled up, leaving but the two sides of the laying-room and roof to be built of lumber; even the roof could be thatched, or earth-covered. All of which could be home-constructed, or by the employment of cheap labor. These habitations would be warmer in winter and cooler in summer, and therefore better than the first described. These quarters, located far enough apart to save the expense of fencing for yards, would save the labor of forage-crops and all meat-food, till the frost cut off the natural supply.

No farmer should be excused from utilizing all such facilities adjacent to his building, which, with the barn-cellar and orchard, would, in most cases, enable him to keep at least two hundred and fifty fowls, all of which could be cared for by the younger members of the family, and the profits would secure older and abler help for the heavier work of the farm, while many a boy would be made a thinking, practical farmer, happy in his lot, who is now chafing under his hard home-life, waiting only for age to liberate him.

Farmers, this poultry-keeping has more than a money value for you. Interest your boys in it, for thereby they learn many of the principles that under-lie the successful breeding of stock,—fitting them, when older, the better to manage cattle and horses. The rapid production of chickens enables them to try as many experiments, in a few years, as would take a lifetime with stock. In the breeding of fowls, they learn that like produces like more surely, and only, as a rule, where the stock is bred in line, and that to produce chickens uniform in type and color, they must have, in both sire and dam, a preponder-ance of the blood of the desired type; they must mate kindred blood judiciously, avoiding too close relationship,—for by mating fowls of one blood for three generations we produce sterility in the egg. They learn that prepotency of sire is more marked in the mating of kindred blood, and in the offspring of dams of weak constitution, and when appearing in the coupling of radically different blood, that it is an exception and not the rule. They learn that the blood most difficult to subjugate, in the end has more lasting quality, and does the flock the most good as a new infusion of blood; these interests, once awaken-ed, cannot slumber; the boys become thoughtful, and, as years increase, you find in them a help not found in your hireling.

So far we have tried to show the best management of adult fowls. But this stock, from year to year, must be renewed; for beyond the second year, younger stock will be found to pay much better, and those birds that are coming two years old in June, should be sold as poultry just before chickens come into the market, when they bring a much better price, and their value will replace them with young stock. If the young stock is to be reared on the farm, it will necessitate the rearing of as many chickens as the breeding-stock number; for chicks hatch nearly equal as to sex, which only enables you to replace the two-year-old birds each year sent to market.

A single brood of chicks will thrive and take care of themselves. With even care, one hundred can be reared in a flock, and all do well. But if more are to be reared, care should be taken to confine those of the same age together,—the February and March chicks in one field, April and May chicks in another, and those hatched later in a third. Each lot will be found to do well; but, if running all together, the young ones get trampled to death by the older ones.

Suppose we should rear our children as many do their chicks, the whole family running over and stepping upon the nursling, should we wonder if it grew up crippled and deformed?

Avoid huddling them together. Twelve to fifteen chicks are all that should be allowed to brood in one coop. We are apt to let the brood quarter in the chicken-coop till quite late in the fall, when they outgrow the coop, and crowding into it, they suffer from their own exhalations ; and the piling one upon another, causes, in many cases, the slipping down of the hips and the one-sided appearance which so often comes to our notice.

The best mode of setting hens is, to sink a barrel on its side one-third into the ground, filling up with earth even with the earth on the outside, using a small quantity of hay to form the nest, especially in early spring. This, you see, will prevent the cold air from reaching the eggs through the hay from the under side, and chilling them, while the earth in the barrel becomes heated by the hen, which increases your chances for an early brood. Place one of the chicken-coops described, in the front of the barrel, and by the means of a slide-door admit the hen to and from the nest. The coop becomes a feeding and dusting yard for her while sitting, and a home for her and her brood when hatched, besides preventing her from deserting her eggs. As the season approaches June and July, pour into the barrel, before putting in the earth, a half-pailful of water. The heat of the hen will draw the moisture up, and prevent too rapid evaporation in the eggs, and secure for you a better hatch.

By setting an even number at a time, and doubling up the broods, you can reset the hens thus released (which generally do better the second time), by which means you secure eighteen clutches of chickens from twelve incubating hens, which will produce as a rule about one hundred to one hundred and ten chickens that will be marketable. The overplus will be found to not more than make good the casualties and deformities.

This plan of hatching and rearing the chickens away from your fowl-houses releases them from, and prevents the incubation of millions of lice, which are generally produced by setting the hens where they are in the habit of laying. If you wish to see every louse and red-spider, which is the same as the bed-bug for the human family, concentrated into twenty inches square, just allow a few hens to incubate in the hen-house. The best food for young chickens, for the first week or ten days, is stale wheat bread, soaked in scalded milk, and occasionally boiled chopped eggs; millet and canary-seed will be found quite forcing, and will give the brood a good start, and it pays to use them for the first two weeks. This feed can be followed by scalded oat-meal, wheat-bran, and corn-meal, mixed, say one-third each, with cracked corn and wheat and whole corn, as soon as the chicks are large enough to eat it.

It is unadvisable to hatch chickens earlier than the season will admit of getting them on to grass by the time they are four weeks old. If they are hatched earlier than this, sow, when the brood hatches, a frame of oats in your hot-house or kitchen, and cut each day the green oats for them. In this way you can carry the chickens over till the grass comes in the spring, and the trouble thus taken will repay you in the possession of early show birds, that generally sell for a much larger price, according to their merit, than later birds; and only by such care can we hope to win the premiums in the September exhibitions. Diarrhœa is the scourge of young chickens in early spring. When the symptoms appear give only scalded milk as drink, and none but cooked food, which will be found generally to correct the evil.

At four to six months old separate the cockerels from the flock, and feed mashed boiled potatoes, with meal and barley and whole corn, thus fitting them for the shambles; and the pullets at five months old place in your breeding-pens, where they will soon commence to repay you for their care, and most assuredly in a like proportion. In nearly all the cases where we find people breeding in this practical way, we find them using only what we call native or mongrel stock. This, we believe, is a mistake, for the thorough-bred is worth as much, and many of the breeds far more, for this practical work; and should all use the thorough-bred, killing as they do now, one-third for poultry, using the larger number left to produce eggs for the market, using as breeders only the best they raise, selling only for breeding purposes when a fair price (say from two dollars and fifty cents to ten dollars each) could be realized, they would in this way raise the standard and come to realize that in every twelve fowls they kept they had the value of a cow, and, caring for them as well, they would find they paid as well.

Show us a farmer who is conscious of capital invested in his fowls, and we will show you a farmer who makes money out of them. The greater the number raised, the higher the price you will be able to command for the best individual specimens. This has proved true in cattle. (See history of Short-horn cattle in America.) It is every day being repeated in fowls. Twenty-five years ago we sold Light Brahmas at one dollar each, and the price was considered a fair one, the native then selling for thirty-three cents. When the price increased to twenty-five dollars per trio, it became the town talk ; but in the past three years, when we have sold cockerels at one hundred dollars, and trios at one hundred and fifty dollars, it has ceased to be a surprise, and really it is not in keeping with bulls at seventeen thousand dollars each. We expect to live to see specimens of superior excellence sold as high as two hundred and fifty dollars. Already, in England, five hundred dollars a trio has been realized.

PART III.

UNIFORM TYPE AND COLOR IN BREEDING.

In setting up your boys in the business of practical poultry keeping, or for breeding thorough-breds for the market, it is well that they have a motive and aim in view,—something that will interest and instruct as well as to make them money. We will therefore give our rule to secure uniform type and coler in breeding, or how to establish a strain of such blood, hoping by interesting them in the theory, to interest them in the practical workings of it.

The American people are lovers of "beauty" in everything; a beautiful horse, a beautiful cow, all demand a price far above those of equal merit that fail in symmetry. Then, in breeding, aim to attain: first, beauty or symmetry; second, color; and both coupled with merit as egg producers ; and as the first two are to be transmitted in a greater degree by the male, it becomes of great importance that he should possess those desirable features.

In selecting a sire, be sure that he is *well bred*, and comes from *a line* of "*good ones,*" a bird which is the counterpart of *his* sire ; for then you have a double guarantee that he will control the offspring. As a rule, the offspring bred back to the grandsire, the sire and grandsire being alike, we start with an almost certainty of success, if we do our part in the mating. Having made our selection, we must put our foot down and stand firmly to the rule of breeding to no sires but this one, or males of his get, and none of them that do not assume the likeness of the sire ; thus establishing a line, or " strain of blood," which, in a single word, means uniformity.

In the hen, secure first, productiveness as to eggs ; second, a robust constitution, coming from a long-lived race ; third, color ; lastly, symmetry : and from this mating select the large pullets that most resemble the sire, and breed them back to the sire. This second crop of birds will be three-fourths the blood of the sire you selected as the founder of your strain.

Now the more stubbornly the blood of the first dam gives up to the blood of the sire, the more good it will do us when subjected properly to him.

Many select well-bred hens of a weakly constitution to make the first cross, for they assert, and truthfully, that the sire being so robust and strong, nearly all the chicks favor the sire. This is all true, but it is also true that the blood used in the hen is weak and will fail in lasting quality. We like strong blood; that which in the first cross seems to fight for the breeding influence; that which has got to be bred back to the strain desired, and the control given if only by a preponderance of blood. We then get a lasting good from the cross. Constitution and vital force must come from the dam, form and color from the sire; and in all the matings, the introduction of new blood must be with a thought to that end.

The crossing of two well-bred strains oftentimes produces a distinct and new type which is very beautiful. To secure this new type (which is in itself a fact that the two elements producing were of equal strength, as neither controlled the breeding), and to perpetuate it, it would in that case be wise to select a dam of delicate though pure

blood, thus giving the sire all the chance possible
to stamp his offspring; then by breeding his pullet
back, to concentrate his breeding in his grand-
children, they also being his children; then we
could go on, by selections of coarser or stronger
dams for new blood for the strain. The American
breeder is of a restless nature; he wants something
that is peculiar to himself; something in which he
can be identified. You find them all over the
country, chopping up the blood of their birds by
the introduction of new sires, first from one flock,
then from another, hoping thereby to have something different. They succeed; but when they have
got it, they are disappointed that no one else wants
it. They think the bottom has gone out of the
chicken business, and they curse the business and
retire. Of such we will say, the business is better
off when they do retire from it. Now, there is
but one way to reach uniformity in breeding, no
matter whether it is horses, cattle, or fowls, and
that is by "in breeding," and, like poison, it may
kill or cure, just according as we display good
judgment in its use.

Whenever we introduce new dams to a strain,
breed their progeny back to the sire of the strain,

and never use sires from this new introduction of blood until the blood has become thoroughly subjected to the strain.

To explain: if the chicks of the mating of the pullets to sires of the strain are not all in type like the strain, then breed back again, and not use a male as a stock bird until the desired affinity of the blood has been accomplished. As a rule, use no male with less than seven-eights of the blood of the strain, nor females with less than three-fourths of the blood of your strain as stock birds.

If all the breeders would adopt this plan of breeding, and would keep a record, they would then see the importance of pedigree, and how beautifully all these things are governed by a natural law. We can mix the blood of our birds as easily as we mix the paints that give us different tints in color. By adhering to this mode, one breeder becomes of benefit to his neighbor breeder; for by crossing strains, the pullets become of equal value to each: each breeding back to his respective strain makes the blood of his neighbor's strain feed the blood of his own. When breeders learn this, and work together, they will all be better off, and may become founders of families in fowls, as now breeders of Shorthorns become in cattle.

PART IV.

DISCUSSION OF THE BOARD.

At the close of the foregoing Essay, the following discussion of the same took place, and we introduce it here on account of its practical import.

Mr. Flint. I have been exceedingly interested in the paper which has been read by Mr. Felch. I am sure he has come up to the expectations of those who had so much confidence, when they invited him to prepare this paper. Mr. Felch has had many years of thorough and careful experience and accurate observation, and I am sure the principles which he has enunciated in his paper will be of great interest and great value to the large number of poultry breeders in this State.

I should very much like to hear the experience and observation of those who are now engaged practically, every day, in poultry breeding. There are a great many questions, I know, that many persons wish to hear discussed, and there are others here who can discuss them better than I can. I have been a somewhat extensive poultry breeder in the course of my life. I have kept a great variety of fowls; too great a variety, altogether, I am sure, for profit. I have generally come to the conclusion, that where profit, for poultry and eggs together, is concerned, the Light Brahma is the best breed; but as egg producers, the White Leghorn, and perhaps one or two other breeds, greatly surpass them.

So far as the feeding of poultry is concerned, I am pretty well satisfied that farmers and those who keep poultry are inclined to feed too much corn. Corn, as you all know, will induce fat, and when poultry are to be fatted for market, they can be fatted, probably, quicker and more economically upon corn or corn-meal, heated, than upon any other substance; but as far as my experience has gone, it is not advisable to feed corn if you wish to get the largest number of eggs; it induces too great fat, especially if the hens are kept in some confinement. Hens that are allowed the whole range of the farm may be fed upon almost anything. They run off what little extra fat they get, perhaps, by eating too much corn; but poultry that are confined, or partially confined, ought not to be fed too much upon corn. Oats, or any of the smaller grains, and vegetables, potatoes, fish, and that class of food, it seems to me, are very much better.

As far as the feeding of fresh or cured rowen or young clover is concerned, I have no doubt that what Mr. Felch has said is correct.

QUESTION. Is there any danger of making White Leghorns so fat by feeding them on corn that they cannot fly?

MR. FELCH. I don't think you can give them anything that will fat them so that they cannot run or fly. But as egg producers, there is no question that the White Leghorn family is the best. They will forage for themselves, and pretty thoroughly, and they are stronger in their feet than the Asiatic breeds, if we are to judge by the damage they will do in the garden.

QUESTION. Do you have bottoms to your coops?

MR. FELCH. I do not. I have simply platforms for early spring, on which to place the coops, in the summer allowing them to set upon the ground.

QUESTION. How do you feed the clover rowen?

MR. FELCH. After curing it becomes brittle; simply feed in a rick, as to stock. If it is cut up too fine, and fed carelessly, they will waste it.

QUESTION. Which is best, the Brown or White Leghorn?

MR. FELCH. I would not say one was better than the other.

QUESTION. Do you have any difficulty in hatching chickens from the eggs that are laid by the Asiatics?

MR. FELCH. That is the danger of the whole business. They sometimes become so very fat, that it will be almost impossible to hatch an egg from them. Turn them right out and give them food that will not fat them, and you will find that the eggs will hatch well.

MR. HERSEY of Hingham. Mr. Felch says that close breeding in and in tends to sterility. I would like to inquire if he has had any actual tests of this, and if so, what difficulties he has encountered.

MR. FELCH. What I mean by in and in breeding is breeding birds of the same blood or pedigree together. I always take pains when I am breeding in line, "breeding in," as I term it, to so mate that there will be a change of blood, and secure the chick in blood different from sire and dam. It is always better to breed back to the sire than to breed the chicks together. When introducing a new element of blood, I find often-times that this works well. This is a rule I have followed for twenty years. I believe I was one of the first to adopt this course. I never buy a male bird, and consequently I have been obliged to make this new blood for scores of others; and when I buy a new bird, I treat it in that way, breeding the pullets of the first cross right back to a sire of that strain, and never use a male bird until I have reduced the foreign blood to one-fourth or one-eighth. Now, if you breed in and in for three generations, that is, breed brothers and sisters, in three generations, it will be almost impossible to hatch an egg.

Mr. Hersey. Have you had any actual tests of it?

Mr. Felch. Yes, sir; I believe, as a rule, the statement I make will hold good. There may be exceptions; there are exceptions to all rules. But I think if any one follows that rule, so that he will know exactly what he is doing, he will find that I am correct. But the fact is, a great many do not know. They will have a flock of birds, and they will save a young cockerel from them and breed from them, thinking they are all of one blood. If they will start from one single dam and breed her chickens together, and their chickens, and then a third lot, I am quite sure they will reach a point where the eggs will not hatch. Unless you have a flock of hens in one inclosure, you can see how easily you lose the track of them. You cannot get uniformity unless you breed your line of sires to the same strain of blood. I think any one who has tried it will agree with me in what I have said on that subject.

Mr. HERSEY. I suppose we meet together here to gather facts, and whatever the result of our experiments may be, it is for our interest to know about them.

Twenty-five years ago, I started for the purpose of demonstrating, one way or another, whether we should be able to breed in and in or not. I took a white native, and from that white native I have bred for twenty-five years, and still the eggs hatch. During the twenty-five years, only three times have I introduced anything different, and those three times it was done by eggs and eggs only, and the male birds were not kept, only the females. But during the last two years, no new blood has been introduced into my flock, and I have bred in and in as closly as possible. And my poultry yard is so situated, and so fenced in, that no other poultry can come near them. Now, the result is, that my eggs hatch a great deal better than my neighbors'. Three years ago (which was the last year that I had the care of them myself), I set four litters, of thirteen eggs each, and every one of them hatched; and of four others, eleven hatched. I think there was not a single litter that year that gave less than six chickens from thirteen eggs.

Now, I admit that I have been careful in breeding to take only those fowls which were physically strong and perfectly healthy. I think that that is a point to which we must look carefully. I believe that healthy birds will bring healthy offspring. But perhaps I ought not to say what I believe. I only rose to state these facts. It is an isolated case, covering a period of about twenty-five years. If there were twenty-five other individuals here who could stand up and say that they had tried the same thing, with the same result, we might be able to come to some correct conclusion. Perhaps a single experiment is not sufficient.

Now, if other people have tried the experiment of in and in breeding, and failed,—if they have really tried it, and not guessed at it,—of course that must count against the experiment which I have made. But I hope that, if this Board shall meet in this or any other hall ten years from this time, there will be many individuals who will be able to rise up and say "I know from practical tests what the result is of breeding in and in."

MR. FELCH. The gentleman who has just taken his seat, says that the introduction of blood was by eggs, saving the females. That does not meet the case, for he put half a dozen new elements into his stock every time he introduced the eggs, which might have helped him out. I do not see that his case touches the point which I advanced, for one introduction of six pullets would have carried him through the whole twenty years, and the eggs would have hatched well.

MR. BILL of Paxton. I have had some experience in keeping hens, but I rise chiefly to add a word to what was said on one point by the gentleman who gave us the very instructive and interesting essay, and that point is this. He spoke of hen-houses in the sides of hills, near our farm buildings, so that the fowls might forage in the pasture with the cattle. Now, he did not state what breed of hen would be the best for that purpose, but I judge from my own experience that a kind of hen not much in favor, perhaps, with most hen fanciers,—I mean the Black Red Game,—is the one best adapted to that purpose.

There is an impression abroad among hen dealers, and those who have not inquired into the matter, that the Black Red Game, or Game hens, are of little value except for their fighting qualities ; but with all my keeping of the Games I never have seen one fight but once, and that was with a White Leghorn, and he got awfully thrashed ; so I am not keeping him for that purpose.   But I find that in the pastures, the Games have the foraging quality, and that is the point I rose to make.   I know tolerably well four or five kinds of Game birds, and any of them will walk off and feed by themselves several hundred rods,—almost a quarter of a mile.

Another notion that is prevalent about them is, that they are quite wild.   That comes partly from the name — *Game.*   But I find that the Games are as gentle, if you treat them gently, as any hens I ever had anything to do with. As to their laying qualities, I have kept them several years, and I am confident that they do lay well. I would not say that they are as good layers as the White Leghorn or the Brown Leghorn, but I do not know any other family, except the Leghorns, that excels the Game in laying qualities.

Another point about the Game is, that their eggs are from a quarter to a third larger than the Light Brahmas', or than almost any of the pure-blooded hens with which I have had anything to do, except the Leghorn.

I would like to ask a question about the Black Spanish. What does Mr. Felch know about them, as to their laying qualities, constitution, etc.?

Mr. Felch. The Black Spanish, before the Leghorn came into notice, was considered the best laying fowl. They lay large eggs, but they do not lay a large number of them. I thing that a full-bred Black Spanish will lay about one hundred and twenty-eight eggs in a year,—about what our native fowls will do. Probably there is not half a dozen eggs a year difference in what the Black Spanish, the Game, and native fowls will lay, and as a rule the Game eggs are much smaller than the Brahma.

QUESTION. How do the Black Spanish stand the cold weather in the winter?

MR. FELCH. Poorly. A Black Spanish chicken is a miserable thing while growing, but when once grown, the fowl seems to be quite hardy. It is a beautiful bird to look at; there is no question about that. If a man does not care how much it costs him to produce and keep a flock of Black Spanish birds, he can have them, and they will do very well, but they are not profitable, managed in a practical way. I tried to find the breed that a person with the least experience could do the best with, everything considered, and that is why I selected the Leghorn, Plymouth Rock and Light Brahma; and here let me say, that, no matter what the breed is, the Almighty has so fixed that thing that they will all pay a profit, if properly managed. A man wants to take the breed that pleases him, and if he does that, he will be likely to take good care of them and make a profit. One man likes the Black Red Game, another the Brown Leghorn, and another the Brahma. I do not agree with those who say that the Buff Cochin is the best bird of the lot. The Buff Cochin is a splendid hen to raise chickens, and they are handy to have for that purpose. They look large, but they are not really so. They are very full feathered, and their feathers make them look large.

Mr. VINCENT. The Black Spanish do not want to sit.

Mr. FELCH. No; but they are of weak constitution. Still, I can hardly say that, because, when once grown, they seem to be hardy, if you can keep them away from the frost. Their wattles and combs are easily chilled, and that seems to take all the life out of them until spring.

QUESTION. What do you consider the best cross?

Mr. FELCH. I consider the best cross in the world is the cross of a White Leghorn cock on a Light Brahma hen. I say a *White* Leghorn, because that cross will produce a uniform white color. There will be no parti-colored feathers, which is an advantage in preparing poultry for the market.

QUESTION. What would be the quantity of eggs produced by that cross?

Mr. FELCH. They will produce as much as either of the thorough-breds. I have birds in my family of Brahmas that have laid for twenty-three successive months without setting; but that is unnatural. I have received several letters this season from parties to whom I have sent birds of this family, stating that their birds have laid the entire season without wanting to set. The Brahmas, both dark and light, do not lay in that way, as a rule.

The Leghorn I call a hardy bird. The Black Spanish I call a delicate bird, because they are predisposed to disease. The whole Spanish class must have dry, warm quarters, or they will have the roup. They will have catarrh in the head, and roup follows, and all the attendant diseases. You cannot put them in a damp place with impunity.

MR. CHEEVER. Is there any limit to the number of eggs that any one of the breeds of hens can lay? I think I have seen it stated in some paper,—from a French authority,—that the ovaries are limited. Do you know anything about that?

MR. FELCH. I do not feel competent to answer that question. I have seen it stated that a hen will not lay after she gets to be four or five years old. But, two years ago, there was a Light Brahma hen at the exhibition in Boston, that was twelve years and three months old, and she laid three days out of the week. I have had a Light Brahma in my yard this year,—eight years old,—and she laid some forty odd eggs. I believe, therefore, that hens will lay until they are pretty old. I do not believe, as some do, that they will cease laying at four or five years of age; but, as a rule, birds, after they are three years old, begin to fall off in the production of eggs.

QUESTION. Are not pullets the most economical kind to keep for eggs?

MR. FELCH. The second year appears to be the year of greatest profit. You may raise two chickens,—a pullet and cockerel,—and the day they are twelve months old, the pullet will have supported herself and the cockerel, and if sold at the end of twelve months, that cockerel is net profit. You may base your calculations of profits upon that, and you will find it to be true. A Leghorn, when she commences to lay, will lay, usually, until she moults, and, generally, will not commence to lay again until the next spring. But you get the start of a year, or longer, before it comes to that, if she has good blood in her.

QUESTION. If you were only keeping a few hens for eggs, what kind would you select?

MR. FELCH. If I were keeping hens for eggs alone, I should most certainly keep the Leghorn breed in preference to any other. Keep the pullets up to the time of moulting, and then sell them and replace them.

QUESTION. Have you had any experience in regard to the laying qualities of the Hamburg?

MR. FELCH. The Hamburg family will lay as many eggs, probably, as the Leghorn. They are handsome birds; and if any one has an eye for beauty, and wants a few handsome birds for eggs alone, I should recommend the Hamburg family. They are a little tender in raising, but, like the Black Spanish, they seem to become hardy afterwards. They lay well. I have had Hamburgs that laid one hundred and fifty-one eggs in six months. That is recorded in the report of the Middlesex South Agricultural Society for the year 1858, and it is also reported, I think, in the State Agricultural Report of that year. The Black Hamburg is, I believe, the best of the family, for their chickens are easily reared, and that, perhaps, is attributable to a cross. I think there is a Black Spanish cross that went into the original Golden Hamburg, that produced the Black Hamburg. The other varieties of the Hamburg family are the Silver and Golden-Spangled and the Silver and Golden-Pencilled. The white and black are two varieties of that class produced within my recollection.

QUESTION. How long do you allow your chicks to run with the hen? Do you have many deformed, one-sided chickens? I am troubled that way.

MR. FELCH. I do not take the hen away until she weans the chicks herself; yet it is as well to remove her to the laying house when the chicks are from five to seven weeks old, according to the season. I have the partings, or slats of my chicken coops, three inches apart, and when my Brahma chicks raise one or both wings to go in or out of the coop, I leave the door open, for in squeezing in and out through the openings between the slats, they easily slip their hips down, thus making them one-sided—deformed—as you have spoken of. I have seen an entire brood ruined by being reared beside a picket fence of one and one-half inch spaces.

The foregoing discussion clearly shows the interest the farmers of the country are taking in this great question of poultry culture. They look upon it from a money point of view. They want to know how many eggs can be produced, and at what cost, and demand practical worth with exhibition excellence.

The rule with all breeds should be, to kill all
the inferior specimens, whether they be male or
female, and demand that the beautiful specimens
be so in a double sense, "Handsome is that, handsome does."

If we breed from none but the most prolific
layers, we shall the more surely improve our stock
in laying qualities. The policy of keeping all the
females, is a bad one; they should be wed out if
they are poor layers.

While the results quoted in the Essay have been
accomplished, and can be again, we can cut down
the figures to a net profit of one dollar per head,
and the margins are then even better than can be
realized upon cattle or horses.

There is no danger of overstocking the market;
for poultry seems to be a necessity. Our Southern
brethren are in a large measure dependent upon it
in warm weather. In all seasons it is to be preferred to beef or mutton and it always rules higher
in the market.

So long as beef, mutton and pork remain at their
present prices, and when (as is the fact,) a pound of
poultry can be raised for the same price per pound,
we see no reason why it will not be a profitable

business. Even in this season of low prices, in other provisions, we find fresh eggs quoted at twenty-seven to thirty cents per dozen, in August, and corn but seventy-five cents per bushel at retail.

A bushel and one peck of corn, or its equivalent, will support a laying hen one year, and if she produces but eleven dozen of eggs, no more than is obtained from the unimproved sort, it will leave a margin of two dollars and thirty-six cents per head for the care of the flock, which would pay, we opine, as well as the majority of the professions.

We would not counsel the use of mongrel stock, as breeders, under any circumstances, nor the use of deformed specimens, only in the case of necessity. Even deformity caused by accident may have so shocked the nervous system as to affect the breeding.

We are knowing to a case where a hen had her foot caught in a steel trap, and, being in it some time before being liberated, had her nervous system so shocked, that after the toes were amputated, five-sixths of the chicks hatched from her eggs the following season, were club-footed in the limb corresponding to the one mutilated on the dam. We know, not all, nor even a very small number of like accidents would produce a similar effect, but we cite the case to show that if an accident can effect the breeding, how much more an hereditary deformity would effect it.

Cross bred fowls are, in the majority of cases, far more prolific as egg producers than the native, or even the thorough-breds from which they were bred, and in all animal or vegetable life this will be found true. Therefore we must always produce them from the two thorough-breds, for to breed from the cross will be to deteriorate.

A few words upon the most fatal and troublesome diseases of poultry and we will leave our readers to breed chickens and be happy.

PART V.

DISEASES OF FOWLS.

We shrink from writing upon this subject, for we are not an M.D., and we only give our views upon, and treatment of a few of the most fatal diseases that we have had occasion to deal with.

We believe in prevention, and when fowls are sick, in extermination, more than in doctoring. When fowls have their liberty they are seldom ill, and when they are confined, if we are careful to furnish a good supply of vegetable food, health generally attends them.

In most of the fatal diseases, there is a poisonous fungus growth in the blood. Fowls never perspire, and the heart beats one hundred and fifty times per minute. The evils that are easily thrown off by perspiration, with them, have to be exhaled by respiration and as a result we find the seat of nearly all the fatal diseases to be in the head, throat, and lungs. Rapid respiration and circulation, therefore becomes necessary to expel the vapory excretions.

The chanticleer of the farm-yard whose liberty is not prescribed, will have a battle every week and not seem the worse for it, while in a similar instance, one kept in a poorly ventilated house, and fed upon unwholesome food will suffer from inflammation and canker, and in very many cases death will follow. And why? Because the blood is poor and even poisoned, and unable to do the work of repairing the damage until it has thrown off the poison from which it is suffering. The former rich in a healthy circulation commences the work of recuperation the moment the wounds of the battle stop bleeding.

We are all aware that iron is one of the very best of blood tonics, and if we but observe, we shall see that fowls kept upon an iron and sulphur charged soil, are generally more healthy and show better lustre to their plumage than those kept upon a dry and arid plain. The reason is that the vegetable growth is but the embodiment of the soils, one furnishing rich iron and sulphur deposits—the other destitute of them.

The breeder if he would be successful will do well to consider his location and furnish artificially that which is lacking in his soil. "From dust and to dust" is true of all things, and it behooves us to see of what kind of dust we build our chickens.

The best doctors are those who watch the patient while well, and prevent sickness, instead of waiting for symptoms and then doctoring them, (the expectant plan, so called,) and finds his remedies in the regulation of the diet.

So the breeder best takes care of his flock, who keeps a watchful eye upon them while at roost. If the droppings from it show a costive tendency, then feed freely of vegetables, such as boiled potatoes, turnips, or cabbage mashed with bran and meal while hot. If the droppings show a relaxed tendency then cease giving vegetables, and resort to baked johnny-cake, corn, and tincture of iron. Sour or sweet milk is one of the best things to feed poultry at all times. Fowls thus carefully fed are seldom sick unless it be that they have what we term the "distemper."

DISTEMPER.

This disease all chickens are heir to, and generally are taken about the time they are from twenty-two to twenty-six weeks old, and at the time they are shedding their second chicken feathers, preparatory to putting on their freedom suits, so to speak.

If carefully watched little or no medicine is needed, and so light is the disease that it hardly deserves a place in this catalogue, yet if not jealously watched it becomes the most frightful in the introduction of roup and consumption.

Symptoms.—A listless quiet mein, a disposition to remain on the roost in the day time, face and comb quite red, and a puff or fullness of the face under the eye. The second day a white froth is discernable in the corner of the eye. A decided loss of appetite is also noticeable.

Treatment.—If noticed, and the disease taken in hand before the appearance of the froth in the eye, it will usually only be necessary to wash the head and beak clean, and blow down through the nose into the throat either with the mouth, or by means of a rubber nipple, thus clearing the tear tube, and bathe the head and wash the throat with a solution of carbolic acid—one part acid to ten parts water. The birds should be kept in a quiet place and allowed nothing but water. The third day they will regain their appetites and all is over. Many of them have this distemper so lightly as not to be noticed.

In aggravated cases when the eyes and face are much swollen, the head and throat should be thoroughly steamed by the use of a large sponge and hot water. The tear tube should be cleared (as before explained,) a desert-spoonful of castor oil given, and the bathing of the face and throat with the solution of carbolic acid continued at short intervals.

This distemper may be called a cold, or the incipient stages of the roup. We will not quarrel about names, but simply say that in our opinion it is no more roup than a cold is measles. There is no offensive smell to the breath as in roup, but if neglected it will excite roup. We have not the slightest doubt of this; in fact know it to be the case, and the breeder has the choice of adopting the adage, "A stitch in time saves nine," and attending to this mild, easily managed distemper, or to neglect it and have that scourge of a poultry house—" THE ROUP"—to contend with.

ROUP.

When roup appears, our advice is, to kill the

affected one and turn your attention at once to the flock, giving sulphur in the ratio of a table-spoonful to fifteen fowls every other day for a week, feeding tincture of iron, eight drops to a hen every day in their soft food, which will pay to be boiled rice, until treatment is over. With this, be sure that the ventilation is complete and free from direct drafts upon the fowls. For the benefit of those who wish to cure the disease we give the following symptoms and our method of treatment :

Symptoms.—Swelling of the head, watery discharges from the eyes and nostrils, which are very fœtid and offensive to the smell, following which, these discharges become acrid and result in a congealed yellow coating to the mouth and tongue, called canker—which we term a poisonous fungus growth in the blood.

Treatment.—Wash and steam the head and throat with hot water in which a dash of carbolic acid is added. Clear the nasal passage to throat by an injection of carbolic water, one part carbolic acid to ten parts water. Gargle the throat and tongue with a solution of potash, but do not peel the canker off, if to do so causes any bleeding, for that would only aggravate the disease. Give a dessert-spoonful of castor oil, and each morning give nearly a gill of milk in which three or four grains of hyposulphite of soda has been dissolved. At evening, after the washing and steaming, the cleansing of the nasal passage, and the gargling, give a gill of milk with eight drops of tincture of iron.

The milk can be easily administered by taking the bird by the under beak and drawing the neck upward till straight, when the milk poured from a tea-pot will run into the crop without the effort of swallowing.

At the end of about four or five days the effect of the hyposulphite of soda in the blood, and the solution of carbolic acid as a wash may be seen in the sloughing off of the cankerous substance from the tongue and mouth, when the fowl will commence to mend. The treatment at this stage should be nourishing food, with occasional doses of sulphur, and the fowls will regain their health and sprightliness.

Six-sevenths of the cases of roup are curable, but its extreme contagion makes the cure a questionable policy, and it should never be undertaken unless the affected fowl be at once removed from the flock and the fowl-house.

CHICKEN POX.

There is a disease, new to us, which came to our notice the present spring, which we should call an eruption, or the chicken pox.

Symptoms.—An eruption of the comb, face and wattles, raised and warty in appearance, and in color a yellowish white. When the crests are removed, these warty substances resemble a bunch of tiny spiles set into the flesh. They bleed profusely.

Treatment.—Remove the crests and bathe in hot water and carbolic acid. When the bleeding ceases apply citrine ointment, when the warts will dry down to a hard black scab. Let the scabs remain for sixty or seventy-two hours, when by removing them, they will take away with them the little white roots of the disease—from one-sixteenth to one-quarter of an inch in length.

Give each morning for four days a pill made as follows: Table-spoonful of common flour, table-spoonful of flour of sulphur, tea-spoonful of cayenne pepper, twenty-five to twenty-eight drops " Fowler's Solution," (if this cannot be obtained, use sixty grains hyposulphite of soda instead,) and milk enough to mould the compound into twenty pills.

Dissolve four grains of quinine in two-thirds of a pint of milk, giving one-half in the morning and balance in evening, or in three equal doses during the day. Feed, while treating, on boiled onions and rice, mixed with oat-meal. If the disease attacks the eye and so prevents feeding, make the food into pellets half the size of one's little finger, which, if dipped in milk and the bird held as described in roup, will slip down the throat readily.

If the sulphur acts too powerfully upon the bowels scald the milk given, which will check its influence on the bowels and cause it to work more strongly in the blood. The disease is so like the "yaws" described by Dr. Quinn, we are of the opinion that it is a kindred one, if not the same.

Roup sometimes accompanies it, but they are not alike. This has a run, and requires from five to seven days to treat it. We tried specimens of a strong constitution by giving milk and water, and without treatment, which recovered. It is very contagious, and on its first appearance kill the specimen afflicted, and by the use of vegetables, sulphur and iron treat your flock to check its spreading. Cleanse the house in which the disease appears as thoroughly as you would a dwelling that had been visited by small pox.

DIPTHERIA.

We give to this new and very fatal disease the above name on account of its symptoms.

Symptoms.—The face and throat become exceedingly red and inflamed; so much so, that if cold water is applied it will evaporate in steam on account of the heat produced by the inflammation. Six hours after this feverish appearance in the throat and face, the throat becomes coated with a yellowish leathery lining, which may be removed by putting down the throat a compressed sponge, liberating it and withdrawing it when it will take up this coating, leaving the surface of the throat a whitish red, thickly studded with minute raw spots from which this poisonous fungus growth seems to exude. If the throat be left without sponging out more than six hours, the coating will adhere to the throat in the same manner as the canker does in roup.

Diarrhœa attends the disease, of a like character to that described in cholera, the discharges resembling a mixture of oil, snuff and chrome green paint.

Exhaustion is very great, so much so that we have given a cock of twelve pounds weight, two ounces of brandy with two ounces of milk in the morning and he showed no evidence of intoxication whatever.

Treatment.—Steam the head and throat with hot water to which a little carbolic acid has been added, and sponge the throat as described in roup, also gargle the throat with a strong solution of potash. (We would obtain from our family physician the same gargles as used for diptheria.)

We have used muriate tincture of iron, touched on the red spots in the throat with a camel's hair brush, which seemed to burn them over and check the leathery fungus growth spoken of. Three grains of hyposulphite of soda in milk in the morning, and three grains of quinine in milk in the evening, together with occasional doses of brandy and raw eggs were used to sustain the life of the fowls while suffering from the disease.

Usually in three days there will be a decided change for the better, or death will ensue.

When the eruption we have called chicken pox accompanied the disease it seemed to act as a counter irritant and more fowls recovered when thus afflicted, than when troubled with the throat disease alone.

In the light of our experience we should not try to save a single specimen but should kill and bury them at once, and attend to the sanitary condition of the remainder of the flock.

The use of Fowler's Solution will be found quite as beneficial, (and in the height of the disease, more so,) as the hyposulphite of soda. One drop morning and evening is sufficient. Should this disease visit one in the form of an epidemic it would be no less, and we are fearful, much more fatal than chicken cholera.

BUMBLE FOOT.

This disease is in very many cases caused by carelessness. Flying down from high roosts to a floor which is always more or less covered by small gravel stones, results in bruises that are precisely like what we usually call " Stone Galls."

The flesh of the foot being so tough, the puss cannot escape, therefore if not attended to, it must congeal, and an ungainly troublesome foot be the result.

The fowl goes lame, and careless of its comfort, we in nine cases in ten fail to investigate in time to prevent serious trouble. When discovered before the puss congeals, lance the swelling at the rear of the foot, and the pressure upon it in walking, will press the puss out and there will be a much smaller callous than if allowed to settle down of its own accord.

We have treated cases by making an incision in front and rear of foot, and those on shank by opening at top and bottom, and by the use of a syringe and a solution of carbolic acid, of one part of acid to ten parts of water, cleanse them thoroughly when they all heal up.

In most cases we are not aware of the trouble till the puss is congealed, when it is almost impossible to press it out unless we take with it some portion of the layers of the foot, which would be worse for the fowl than to use a strong liniment to take out the soreness, and let the inflammation settle down into a corn.

When the swellings are upon the shank or knee-joints which are generally the result of rheumatism, or gout, the fowl may as well go to the block, for it is a doubtful policy to breed from such a specimen.

But some have a mania for doctoring, in which case use strong liniment, and bind the shanks and joints in leaves or bulbs of the skunk cabbage, and give internally, one drop, morning and night, of "Fowler's Solution" for a month, or bromide of potash, three grains per day until the trouble is cured.

Bumble foot may be prevented in a great degree by providing low roosts and keeping the floor of the fowl-house covered three inches deep with loamy sand, which costs less than to doctor fowls for the want of it.

THE RED SPIDER LOUSE.

This pest is the scourge of the poultry-house, and the source of more trouble and annoyance than any other hindrance to poultry keeping. The quarters often become literally alive with them before the breeder is aware of their presence. They sap the life blood from the fowls and reduce to skeletons and debilitate a flock to such an extent, as to make the season unprofitable. Working only in the night, they escape notice and have things their own way.

Fowls that are sitting upon eggs are generally the greatest sufferers, for these lice instinctively seek out such hens as are about to hatch their broods, and many a hen sacrifices her life to her mother-hood.

In this case the hen becomes sallow in face and comb—actually bloodless, the lice having consumed the blood to such an extent as to cause death, and many fowls, whose deaths have been attributed to disease, have been murdered by these pests.

The quarters should be constantly watched, and all the cracks and knots, on or about the roosts, saturated with coal tar and kerosene oil, or carbolic acid. The houses must be kept free from them, for the exhaustive influence of these maurauders not only entails the loss of blood to the fowls, but by reducing their strength, renders the flock more liable to the diseases we have described.

It is therefore the best and surest step toward warding off disease, to have an absolutely clean poultry-house. If from one to three pounds of sulphur be mixed with the loamy sand and gravel covering the floor, in which the fowls may dust themselves, and kerosene oil used as described, the fowls occasionally dusted while on their roosts with a dredging box filled with sulphur and Persian insect powder, or carbolic powder, their quarters will soon be cleansed.

Cleanliness coupled with judicious feeding is what makes fowls profitable. So great a nervous irritant are these species of vermin, that in two flocks equally well fed, the flock which occupies quarters infested with lice will not lay at all, while those free from this annoyance will lay nearly every day. This fact proves them to be an expensive enemy to the poulterer.

We do not go so far as some writers, and say that all disease is caused by lice, but will say that many a fowl would not have suffered disease, were it not for this barn or spider louse. Breeders, look for them at all times. Do not wait for them to make themselves known, and force their acquaintance upon you.

PART VI.

SPECIFIC FOOD FOR FOWLS.

A few words upon the use of the several condiments advertised for fowls or egg production may not prove amiss in this work.

In most cases, where these condiments are needed, the breeder is troubled to obtain a variety of food for his flock. We have demonstrated the necessity of the daily use of flesh, vegetable and grain food, and where the meat and vegetable elements are lacking, their constituent parts have to be supplied in a concentrated form. Thus sulphur and iron become a necessity, and want of time to supply in their natural form all the elements of food that are necessary, has caused a large demand for these specific foods and condiments for fowls. Therefore a word of direction for their use will prove advantageous.

Of the many kinds now in use, it is safe to say that in all are found nearly the same ingredients,— the quantity of each in the compounding, being the greatest difference in them. These condiments and egg foods should be carefully administered. No general rule can be followed. One should begin with less than directed, and increase the quantity until the desired result is accomplished.

We have, in testing some of the egg foods, given them as directed, and forced some of the fowls to lay three soft shelled eggs in a single night, two hens side by side producing five such eggs in a night. It is evident then, that in such doses the food becomes abortive.

Breeding fowls should not be allowed to lay more than one hundred eggs in the six months termed the breeding season, and if they are found to be falling off from that ratio, the food may be used to stimulate them to a natural production, or over fat fowls may be induced to lay more freely by its use, and their fat reduced to some purpose.

Fowls kept to produce eggs for the market, may be fed upon this food more freely until they are forced up to their full constitutional limit, and when moulting time arrives, they may be killed and marketed for poultry. Birds thus forced will generally moult slowly, and fail to lay till the following spring, which would make it more profitable to replace them with young stock that will stand the use of the food, and pay a profit on its use.

To be able to use fowls for a series of years, the egg production should be the result of proper food. We have had our attention directed to a preparation called "Animal Meal," composed of fresh meat, fresh bone, and carbonized grain, which to our mind is a desirable food for fowls. We are all aware of the healthful properties of charcoal for fowls, and especially for fattening turkeys for the market.

The carbonizing of the grain gives all the properties of charcoal, while it retains all the nutriment of the grain, and being ground into a meal with the meat and bone, preserves them sweet for general use. Thus we have a feed which, if mixed in the ratio of one part animal meal, three parts bran, and three parts corn-meal, or with six or eight times its bulk of meal or coarse food, and made into a warm mash for the morning meal, is highly nutritious, and yet as cheap as ordinary grain.

Its use in conjunction with the chemical egg powders would augment the influence of both, and the fowls could be forced to their utmost limit. In feeding these stimulants the vegetable diet must not be neglected.

In leaving the subject in the hands of our readers, we hope they will not condemn, until they have first put the suggestions herein contained into practice, when we shall feel that they, like the author, will have accomplished good results.

APPENDIX.

HENRY F. FELCH'S POULTRY-HOUSE.
(SEE FRONTISPIECE.)

We give as a frontispiece the cut of a poultry-house erected by H. F. Felch which is peculiarly adapted to the needs of the poultry breeder.

For the benefit of those who would like to erect a handsome, durable, and convenient poultry-house, we give its dimensions, also a plan of the ground floor, and second story.

FIRST STORY—40 feet x 20 feet.

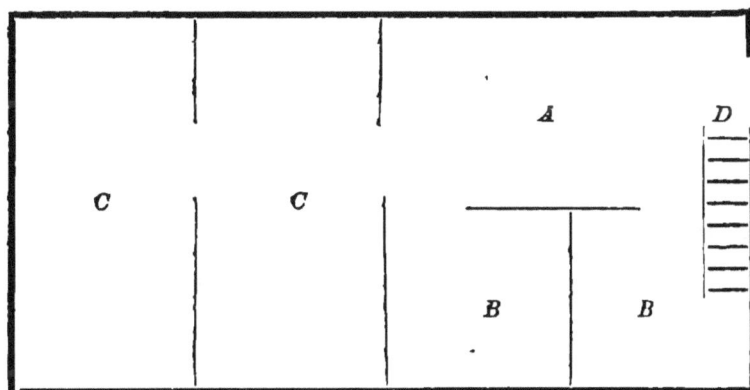

A, entry and grain room, 10 x 20 feet. *B B* rooms 10 x 10 feet, for breeding stock. *C C* a room each for pullets and cockerels—general stock. *D* stairway to second story.

SECOND STORY.

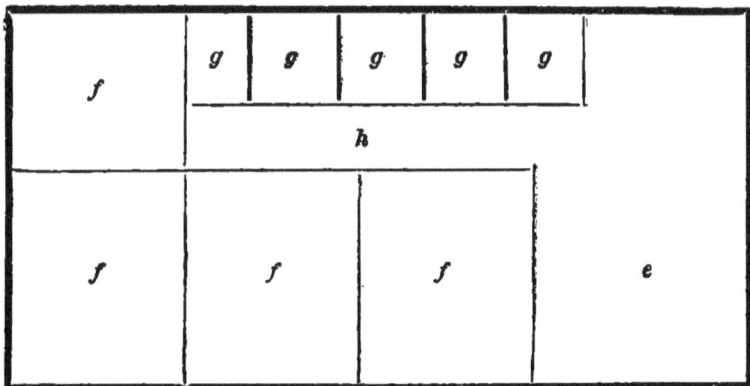

E store room—*f f f f* four rooms for sitting hens or hens and chickens, *g g g g g* five small rooms for single cocks, or for sitting hens, *h* passage.

The form and general appearance of the building is shown in the cut. The partitions are made of wire netting, giving a roomy, pleasing appearance, as well as affording light and ventilation.

We think the building would be improved by slightly increasing its height—say to 12 feet in the posts, and inserting double windows in the gables, which would give a window in each of the large rooms of the second story.